Some Day Peace Will Return
NOTES ON WAR AND PEACE

Some Day Peace Will Return

❦ NOTES ON WAR AND PEACE

Arthur Schnitzler

EDITED AND TRANSLATED,
WITH AN INTRODUCTION, BY
Robert O. Weiss

Frederick Ungar Publishing Co., New York

Translated from Arthur Schnitzler's
Und einmal wird der Friede wiederkommen
and published by arrangement
with S. Fischer Associates, Inc.

Copyright © 1972 by
Frederick Ungar Publishing Co., Inc.
Printed in the United States of America
Library of Congress Catalog Card Number: 78-158407
Designed by Irving Perkins
ISBN 0-8044-2803-4

Contents

Introduction 1

Some Day Peace Will Return 33

Editor's Notes 97

Introduction

❦ Arthur Schnitzler is no stranger to lovers of good plays and good literature. His name was familiar even to those of his contemporaries who never attended the theater or read anything but the newspaper, for Schnitzler was also a controversial figure during much of his lifetime. This unwanted distinction came to him because he was guilty of two sins of the truly great: he was far ahead of his time in his social and scientific thinking, and he fought an unrelenting battle for his right to tell the truth as he saw it. His steadfast opposition to hypocrisy, incompetence, falsehood, and any degradation of human dignity earned him the hatred of those enemies of truth and progress who thrive on mediocrity and stereotyped thinking.

Others, of course, have taken a similar path and have suffered similarly for pursuing it. But most of them were more judicious in the choice of their enemies and more careful not to alienate their followers. Schnitzler had no wish for disciples—at least not in the conventional sense— and his few intimate friends welcomed, rather than were offended by, his uncompromising honesty.

Through his efforts to unmask the motives of those who had an interest in and worked for the perpetuation of certain deplorable social and political conditions, Schnitzler exposed himself to bitter animosity and malicious slander. The most violent of his detractors were not, indeed, those who misunderstood him; rather they were those who understood him only too well. The odds were strongly in their favor. Collectively, they commanded the strategic advantages that Schnitzler lacked: power, influence, unscrupulousness, the subservience of the censors, and access to the means of reaching the public. Schnitzler had one weapon and one defense: the truth and his own incorruptibility, coupled with his literary genius. In later years he could add to these the loyalty of his friends.

Among his enemies there were some whose techniques were infamous. Nothing base was missing from their arsenal: the big lie and the half-truth, the innuendo, the whispering campaign, anti-Semitism, forgery, misrepresentation, perjury, paid agitators, riots.

At the appearance of *None but the Brave* (*Leutnant Gustl*, 1900),* for example, the publication *Vaterland* called the work "This mixture of offal, lowest mentality and depravity of the heart, of cowardice and unscrupulousness." The *Österreichische Volkspresse*, which catered to low-brow readers, commented about the work: "all the other trashy products of this Jew [Schnitzler]. . . . We say 'our army' because it . . . is an out-and-out Aryan one, therefore

---

* The following quotations are from "Schnitzler and the Military Censorship: Unpublished Correspondence" by Otto P. Schinnerer (*Germanic Review*, V, 244–245). Translations are mine.

strictly counter to Jewish nature and thoroughly hateful to the Hebrews."

In a similar manner the *Kikeriki* published not only strongly anti-Semitic cartoons of Schnitzler and an article entitled "Aaron Schnitzler," but even "poetry" such as this:

Lieutenant Gustl, who by Schnitzler
Is presented as a coward
Bare of courage and of honor
And who shows himself a shirker:
Was he not himself a Jew,
Just as Schnitzler is and will be?
And if so, then why complain
If one Jew describes another?

As for *Hands Around* (*Reigen*, 1900),* one reviewer substituted such expressions as "the well-known Jewish stink" and "canine lubricity" for objective judgment. The critic for the Munich newspaper *Allgemeine Zeitung* resorted to outright falsification and an obscene analogy when he stated that Schnitzler "shows jeeringly that even Romeo and Juliet were basically only a lewd scoundrel and a stupid prostitute! It is as if he had a pair of dogs copulate before a statue of Aphrodite."

By their actions one can see how very important it was to certain elements that the voice of Arthur Schnitzler be discredited, if not silenced —and awareness of this fact may alert the reader to the deeper significance of his works.

---

* The following quotations are from "The History of Schnitzler's *Reigen*" by Otto P. Schinnerer (*Publications of the Modern Language Association*, XLVI, 840, 843). Translations are mine.

Unfortunately, Schnitzler's enemies succeeded to some extent. Through propaganda tricks, they managed to distort his literary image, to portray him as only a moderately gifted writer without depth or lasting significance. Thus, for decades, they did their best to prevent his work from gaining the recognition it deserves.

On the other hand, in spite of everything done to denigrate him, Schnitzler was one of the most famous men of his day—though he cared little enough for that status. Although some of his plays and books were variously proscribed, the ban was eventually lifted.

In recent years, the admiration of competent critics, Germanists, literary historians, and discerning laymen has resulted in a Schnitzler renaissance that has brought about a reevaluation and a better appreciation of Schnitzler's writings. His greatest victory has been awarded him by the judgment of time: Schnitzler's work has indeed survived.

Many writers, such as Thomas Mann, have paid tribute to Schnitzler's great literary talents. An example of such admiration is the following comment by Hugo von Hofmannsthal:

> At his service are all the tools that artisanship places in the hands of an experienced and very reflective artist to enable him to master even substance that is apparently unmalleable and to elicit from the subject its inner riches. None of them does he use with greater and more charming virtuosity than irony. The more boldly he applies it, the more he forces his material and his motives into a corner with it, all the broader, paradoxically, his intellectual ho-

rizon seems to be. Thus I would say that, next to *Liebelei*, a work of an entirely unique kind, several of his *small* works of art—tales and plays—emerge, through the magic of irony, as his greatest.

Schnitzler is now greatly admired for his artistically superb dramas, short stories, and novellas and for his astonishing grasp of depth psychology revealed in them.

Even so, his aphoristic and essayistic writings are still all too little known. The works *Der Geist im Wort und der Geist in der Tat* (1927) and *Buch der Sprüche und Bedenken* (1927) appeared after he had been famous for many years as a dramatist and author of narrative fiction. Once the image of a public figure is established, it is not easily amended. In this age of specialization, neither the artistic efforts of a scientist nor the scientific work of an artist is likely to be taken seriously, whatever their merit. This may explain why Schnitzler's sociophilosophical publications were issued in small printings and allowed to go out of print. Most copies were destroyed in the book-burning during the years of Nazi barbarism, and the few extant copies of Schnitzler's philosophical writings became rarities.

Now both these books, along with *Some Day Peace Will Return: Notes on War and Peace* (*Und einmal wird der Friede wiederkommen*) and other previously unpublished writings, are collected in *Aphorismen und Betrachtungen*, edited by Robert O. Weiss, which is Volume V of Schnitzler's Collected Works (Frankfurt: 1967).

English translations of these writings, to the

best of my knowledge, have not hitherto been published, though selections from *Some Day Peace Will Return*, as well as a number of aphorisms, appeared in two American periodicals. The English translation of *Der Geist im Wort und der Geist in der Tat* as *The Mind in Words and Actions* is being published at this time. A translation of *Buch der Sprüche und Bedenken* as *Reflections and Aphorisms* is being prepared.

ARTHUR SCHNITZLER: A PROFILE

Schnitzler repeatedly expressed his conviction that an artist gives only his work to the public but owes no accounting of any part of his private life. It is understandable, then, that little authentic information on Schnitzler was available in his lifetime. Lately more data have emerged, such as his fragmentary memoirs, *My Youth in Vienna*,* but the total remains inadequate for biographical purposes. This situation is not likely to improve soon, since his extensive diaries will not be made accessible to the public in the foreseeable future.

Arthur Schnitzler was born on May 15, 1862, in Vienna, the then still glamorous capital of the Austro-Hungarian monarchy and a major cultural center of Europe. As a son of the renowned laryngologist and university professor

---

* *Jugend in Wien*, ed. by Therese Nickl and Heinrich Schnitzler (Vienna: 1968). Translated by Catherine Hutter (New York City: Holt, Rinehart, & Winston, 1971). This work includes very little beyond the year 1889.

Dr. Johann Schnitzler and of a mother who was a member of the prominent Markbreiter family, Schnitzler began life in secure and comfortable circumstances. This good fortune assured young Schnitzler an excellent education and spared him the economic woes that plagued other outstanding writers of his era. On the other hand, Schnitzler was born a Jew into a society with a formidable tradition of anti-Semitism. Although not conventionally religious, indeed strongly opposed to the orthodox and the doctrinaire, Schnitzler never denied his Jewishness and thus remained throughout his writing years a target of bigotry.

Whether one thinks of Schnitzler as a writer who had been a physician or as a physician who became a writer, both vocations had their origin in his home. His decision to study medicine was based primarily on his desire to please his father. His brother Julius (1865–1939) also studied medicine and became an outstanding surgeon and director of the Vienna City Hospital. On the other hand, the many famous artists, especially the actors and singers, among his father's patients stimulated the boy's interest in music as well as his attempts at writing, which he began at the age of nine. Indeed, prior to the completion of his *Anatol* cycle, in 1891, he had finished more than two dozen plays, some fifteen narrative works, and a number of poems. These juvenilia, however, did not indicate an extraordinary talent. Schnitzler himself was later to rate them as artistically worthless—a judgment that seems rather harsh in some instances.

In 1885 Schnitzler received his medical degree

from the University of Vienna. In 1893, having completed additional clinical training as well as his obligatory service as an army doctor, he began to practice medicine. He soon became dissatisfied, not with the profession itself, but with the medical establishment, with the incompetence and cynicism of so many of its practitioners. Increasingly he realized that he was not suited to practice medicine.

Furthermore, his primary medical interest focused on a specialty that then existed only as a stepchild of neurology: psychiatry. Independent of other pioneers in the field, e.g., Charcot and Bernheim in France or, for that matter, Freud in Vienna, Schnitzler did substantial experimental work and research on hypnosis, especially on hypnotherapy of what we now know as conversion hysteria. Subsequently, like Freud himself, he went far beyond the primitive "psychiatry" of his time and, again quite independently, arrived at some concepts of depth psychology very similar to those of Sigmund Freud. Some of these cognitions actually preceded Freud's own.

After his father's death in 1893, Schnitzler began to devote more time to his literary endeavors. Increasingly, he had been restricting his medical activities, until in 1894 he had ceased to accept new patients. His writings, however, contain ample confirmation of his statement that, for him, medicine was a philosophy, a way of thinking and feeling that he could never abandon.

Outwardly, Schnitzler's life as a young man differed little from that of his peers—full of activity and lighthearted love affairs. Yet these were truly years of apprenticeship for him—years of exuberance as well as sadness, of growing up through experimenting, of self-doubt and self-discovery.

Having enjoyed the pleasures of youth to the fullest, Schnitzler abandoned that phase in due course. By 1891, now a serious intellectual, he belonged to the so-called Young Vienna group of writers, would-be authors, critics and avant-garde publishers, presided over by the flamboyant Hermann Bahr. This quite loosely knit group, meeting casually in the now long-gone Café Griensteidl, constituted no literary school or movement. Those who participated in the Griensteidl gatherings had really just one thing in common: the desire to revitalize Austrian literature. Each one worked toward this end in his own way—some, like Hugo von Hofmannsthal, with eminent success. Schnitzler, too, was now on the road to literary fame, and from here on his writing would dominate his life.

Reminiscences of contemporaries of the mature Schnitzler convey the impression of a sociable, well-liked person. In the evenings Schnitzler could often be found in the Cafehaus unter den Arkaden, engaged in the serious or humorous discussions he so much enjoyed. His genuine good humor, it is said, enlivened the nightly meetings at the café. His compelling sincerity and honesty inspired such confidence that sometimes even casual acquaintances opened their hearts to him. The great conductor Bruno Walter told me that Schnitzler radiated kindness of heart combined with strength of character. This seems to be the prevailing sentiment though the German novelist Jakob Wassermann notes that Schnitzler tended to be somewhat impatient with minds less agile and disciplined than his own.

Almost reverently Schnitzler's friends remember in their reports his generous hospitality, the pleasant hours spent at his home, his stimulating personality. Schnitzler, it is true, did not encourage easy familiarity, even from the members of his inner circle, but his reserve was hardly that of a snob. Indeed, in the published memoirs of those who knew him, there is abundant evidence of their deep affection and respect for this unpretentious man who ranks among the great literary figures of his time.

While interested in, and highly appreciative of, all the fine arts, Schnitzler loved music best. Bruno Walter once mentioned to me that he had never met anyone with more appreciation and understanding of music than Schnitzler.

In 1903, Schnitzler married Olga Gussmann, the mother of his then one-year-old son, Heinrich, and in 1909 his daughter Lili was born. Thereafter, the fates were to allow him only a few more years of relative peace.

In these years, when Schnitzler was approaching the peak of his intellectual maturation and artistic creativity, his world was coming to its end. The agony started in 1914, and when it was over, an irreplaceable part of Western civilization lay dead. As World War I destroyed the world that Schnitzler knew and loved so well, it wrought major changes in him too. His essential optimism—now gone forever—was replaced by a growing conviction that not a phoenix but a vulture would arise from the ashes of European civilization.

It is significant that Schnitzler never published any play or narrative that touched upon the cataclysm of World War I. He would not use his art to probe in the wound that burned in his soul as long as he lived.

He also refused to recognize the ugly postwar realities in his subsequent writings, in spite of, or perhaps because of, his great ability to empathize. Nevertheless, creative work was indispensable to Schnitzler, and so he continued to devote himself to his writing. His ripest, finest work stems from this period of his life. Among these works are: the magnificent novellas *Casanova's Homecoming* (*Casanovas Heimfahrt*, 1918) and *Fräulein Else* (1924); the collection of aphorisms *Reflections and Aphorisms* (1927); the important sociophilosophical study *The Mind in Words and Actions* (1927); and the novella *Flight into Darkness* (*Flucht in die Finsternis*, 1931), a masterpiece of psychiatric insight and novelistic skill. He chose, however, to draw his settings and characters without exception from the prewar era.

This fact as well as Schnitzler's self-imposed loneliness seems to indicate that he made a withdrawal-type adjustment to the self-styled brave new world that did not impress him as being so brave. He could not tear out by the roots his heart, spirit, and intellect, his concepts of beauty and truth—all deeply anchored in the past—in order to transplant himself into an epoch in which he may have discerned already the seeds of the even more frightful holocaust that lay ahead. Thus Schnitzler turned back to his own time and continued to write fine, sensitive narratives and plays, filled with tender beauty, much wisdom, and a great deal of disconsolate sadness.

His increasing withdrawal from a formerly active social life was not due exclusively to the shattering effects of World War I but to some extent to a hearing loss that made him avoid social gatherings. The degree of his auditory impairment seems to have been relatively moderate. But to Schnitzler it was a major calamity because it also impaired significantly his enjoyment of music.

In Schnitzler's last years he was not spared personal tragedy. His marriage had ended in divorce in 1921, and in 1930 his beloved daughter committed suicide. The grief-stricken Schnitzler survived her by only one year. In earlier years he had also known grief. In 1894 he met Maria Reinhard whom he came to love deeply. Five years later he, a physician, had to stand by helplessly when she died from peritonitis.

Schnitzler, though still gracious and kind, became increasingly reticent as the years went on. In April 1931, the German novelist Jakob Wassermann visited him for the last time. According to him, Schnitzler seemed outwardly unchanged. His emotional condition, however, caused some concern to Wassermann, who found Schnitzler depressed and no longer trying to hide that fact. He was embittered and saddened by what he saw as the intellectual and spiritual decay of the postwar world. Yet, immersed in melancholy as he was, Schnitzler still treated Wassermann to "the most amusing conversation imaginable, full of sparkle and of surprising turns." Six months later, Schnitzler died at the age of sixty-nine.

One of the most significant tributes to Schnitzler stems from Bruno Walter, who said during a conversation we had in 1959: "Arthur Schnitzler's impression upon me was so profound that he has become infinitely more than a memory: he is an inseparable part of myself. Had I not known him, I'd be a totally different person."

SOME OF SCHNITZLER'S WORK AND THOUGHT
AS INDICES OF HIS DEVELOPMENT

Good English translations of Schnitzler's works are virtually nonexistent. Still, his name is known in this country, mainly because several of his plays—such as *The Game of Love* (*Liebelei*, 1894) or selections from the *Anatol* cycle of one-acters (published in book form, 1893) — have remained perennial favorites of the amateur stage, and because the highly successful French motion picture *La Ronde* was a screen version of his *Hands Around* (*Reigen,* 1900).

This limited, nonrepresentative exposure has made it all but impossible for the American public to evaluate the uncomprehending or malicious judgment of the critics prior to World War II, who habitually misrepresented Schnitzler in terms of disparaging stereotypes. In many minds he has therefore remained the poet of Viennese decadence, of moral relativism—an arch-impressionist without depth, though amusing in a quaint sort of way.

A prime factor in the perpetuation of these erroneous opinions has been what might be termed the "inertia of criticism"—a tendency to classify and label an emerging author, and then, with a tenacity proportionate to the incorrectness of the initial evaluation, to ignore all evidence of subsequent growth, maturation, or change. Indeed, Schnitzler's true worth might have been acknowledged decades sooner if his early works had found less acclaim and had thus escaped the distorting stereotyping of the critics.

Actually, Schnitzler attained considerable fame long before World War I because his early writings were the kind of literature evidently liked and wanted by the public: some frivolous gaiety, seasoned with a little melancholic nostalgia and spiced with witty dialogue. In the last decade of the nineteenth century, however, Schnitzler found his artistic stride and soon turned away from this phase of his work with its emphasis on the entertaining *süße Mädel* and "frivolous melancholics"—Viennese types from a vanishing era. (The literal translation—sweet girls—does not convey the special meaning that the German *süße Mädel* had for Schnitzler's contemporaries. To them, the term referred to girls of the lower classes—working girls from the outskirts of Vienna—whose longing for some romance and a little glamour in their dreary lives was often exploited by the well-to-do young men of the middle and upper classes. The *süße Mädel* were fair game to these men—pleasant and convenient partners for fleeting love affairs, but never to be even thought of in terms of marriage.) Instead, he embarked on a perilous course of "telling it as it is," a course dictated by his love of truth and by his expanding social conscience.

In 1896 he had published *Free Game* (*Freiwild*), a play that infuriated reactionaries and militarists with its attack upon the practice of dueling and on certain aspects of the social caste system with its peculiar code of honor. Yet Schnitzler ignored ominous reactions in influential circles that he had aroused with this play. On Christmas Day of 1900 his *None but the Brave* (*Leutnant Gustl*) appeared in print, a novella (using the interior monologue, a technique new to German fiction) that satirized the dubious honor concept of a young army officer and again pointed out the absurdity of dueling. This time the guardians of the status quo reacted fiercely. Chauvinistic and anti-Semitic elements heaped poisonous abuse on Schnitzler, and the military establishment reacted officially by revoking his commission as a medical officer in the Austrian Army Reserve. In time, the anti-Schnitzler campaign lost its edge, but Schnitzler was henceforth outside the pale not only for the bigots and chauvinists, but also for many conservatives.

Equally outspoken social criticism is expressed in the play *The Legacy* (*Das Vermächtnis*, 1899). It conveys strong condemnation of the hypocrisy and arrogant intolerance among the upper middle classes. This drama, with its collection of despicable hypocrites, also invalidates the claim of some critics that Schnitzler's characters are too vapid to evoke any strong emotional responses. The reader of *The Legacy* responds with as much outrage against the sanctimonious Professor Losatti and the sadistic, holier-than-thou Dr. Schmidt as he is likely to feel toward any fictional figure.

A wider range of social injustice is castigated in the five-act play *Professor Bernhardi* (1912) and in the novel *The Road to the Open* (*Der Weg ins Freie,* 1908). In these works Schnitzler draws attention to the self-serving manipulation of public opinion by unscrupulous politicians and pressure groups, as well as to anti-Semitism and other ills of society.

An important sociopsychological question is raised, though not explicitly answered, in the short story "The Son" ("Der Sohn," 1892) and in the novel *Theresa: The Chronicle of a Woman's Life* (*Therese: Chronik eines Frauenlebens,* 1928). Is it conceivable that, in special circumstances, a murderer (the son) is less to be blamed for his crime than his victim (the mother)? Can experiences in earliest infancy, such as a drastic act of maternal rejection or adverse environmental conditions, be the hidden causes of the violent, senseless crimes of the psychopath?

In the first decade of this century Schnitzler turned to other themes. He handled what appear to be preternatural and parapsychological phenomena in the one-act play "The Lady with the Dagger" ("Die Frau mit dem Dolche," 1902) and the short stories "The Fate of Baron von Leisenbohg" ("Das Schicksal des Freiherrn von Leisenbohg," 1904), "The Prophecy" ("Die Weissagung," 1907), and "Redegonda's Diary" ("Das Tagebuch der Redegonda," 1911). In these, and other works that involve the preternatural, Schnitzler, who was fascinated by the mysterious nature of reality, carefully leaves open the possibility that the phenomena described could have occurred by chance or through natural causes. Throughout Schnitzler's work run the ever-recurring themes of the essential loneliness of the individual, of man's inability to fully understand—let alone to completely "own" —another human being, of existential anguish, of the nature of truth and reality, of life and death.

Through the medium of psychology Schnitzler observed the complex manifestations of human emotions and behavior, then conveyed to his readers what he had found.

As one might expect, Schnitzler's great interest in depth psychology and psychopathology is prominently reflected in his literary work. In addition to almost all major types of psychoneurotics, there are over thirty psychotic figures in his fictional writings—so accurately presented that many of them could be used as paradigms of present-day psychiatric theory. The novella *Flight into Darkness*, published the year of his death, is an example of this. At first reading, the wealth of psychiatric material in it is hardly noticed because this work attracts the reader through the skillful unfolding of the plot line and the exemplary style. One sees that Robert, the central figure, is gradually losing his mind, but not that a detailed clinical history of an individual suffering from paranoid schizophrenia could be assembled from this work. This fidelity to the authentic is generally characteristic of Schnitzler's writing.

Schnitzler's range of subjects, it can be seen, greatly exceeds the scope of his early writings. It is similarly true that his style varied broadly beyond his early works.

The practice of classifying Schnitzler as an out-and-out impressionist is erroneous. While several of his better-known works are indeed written in an impressionistic manner, he also employed techniques of other literary movements. For example, because of the strong social criticism and the way in which the plots are developed, *The Legacy* and *Free Game* reveal characteristics of naturalism. *Theresa,* too, has many features of a late-naturalistic novel.

The puppet play *Zum großen Wurstl* 1905—untranslated) is a model of expressionistic technique: the characters have no names or personal identity. "The gay person," "The sarcastic person," "The unknown person," "The well-meaning person," "The verbose person," "The naive person," and others—all are symbolic figures, representing not individuals, but types and ideas.

Romanticism in the works of Schnitzler can be easily pinpointed. He frequently used the typically romantic vehicle of the fairy tale, particularly when he wanted to express philosophical ideas without relating them to a specific time or social stratum. Thus the ideological cores of the short stories "Die drei Elixiere" (1894—untranslated), "The Triple Warning" ("Die dreifache Warnung," 1911), "The Shepherd's Pipe" ("Die Hirtenflöte," 1911), and "Legende" (1932

—untranslated) are cloaked in the language and atmosphere of the fairy tale. The longing for, and the pursuit of, the unattainable—essential ingredients of German romanticism—are also evident in these stories. They all reflect man's eternal quest to understand the incomprehensible, or his tragic attempts to acquire powers that are denied human beings. The mystical—another prominent element of romanticism—is present not only in these stories, but also in the works in which Schnitzler includes preternatural phenomena. Romantic irony is evident in *Zum großen Wurstl,* in spite of some expressionistic features. Here "The Poet" satirizes his work as well as himself. *Weltschmerz* (a form of existential despair)—another attribute of German romanticism—is exemplified in the motives for the suicide of the poet Filippo Loschi in Schnitzler's great Renaissance drama *Der Schleier der Beatrice* (1901—untranslated).

An analysis of Schnitzler's *Weltanschauung* reveals that he was fascinated by the subject of truth, especially its elusive properties and its relation to falsehood. In *The Big Scene* (*Große Szene,* 1915), the actor Konrad Herbot deceives Edgar Gley about his relationship with Gley's betrothed, Daisy, by means of a half-truth. Everything Herbot says to Gley is objectively true, but his words become lies because of what he omits to say. Herbot shows Gley a letter from Daisy that is genuine enough, but it is deceptively used because it was written earlier than Gley is led to assume, written before Daisy had become Herbot's mistress. Many other examples of the relativity of truth can be found in

Schnitzler's works, and his skepticism may have resulted from his preoccupation with truth.

But that same preoccupation may have led him to become distrustful of his own skepticism and to eventually conclude that truth ultimately must be anchored to absolute ethical values and personal responsibility. The transition from Schnitzler's early moral relativism to his rejection of its tenets in his last years was a gradual one. His philosophical development was reflected in his characters. He did not suddenly start to create moral paragons. The change, though significant, was subtle. Formerly the central characters in Schnitzler's works, such as Anatol, incurred only superficial adversities as a result of their amoral philosophy and behavior, while Schnitzler seemed to be viewing them tolerantly. Later, similar figures suffer tragic consequences, as Schnitzler makes the point that unbridled hedonism is not a key to life or a way to attain happiness. One need only think of his Erasmus and Dionysia in "The Shepherd's Pipe."

In this story Erasmus has intellectualized himself into extremes of amoral philosophy, to the point of forcing his wife Dionysia to leave their home in order "to fulfill her destiny," as Erasmus describes it. Throwing herself into one episode after another, Dionysia experiences the greatest ecstasies and the deepest despair. But when, from her strange journey, she returns to the man who had sent her away and absolved her in advance of her actions, she cannot bear to stay with him. So complete is his amorality that he asks no questions, being genuinely uninterested in the details of Dionysia's odyssey. He is ready to resume their former life, as if nothing had happened. Dionysia, however, is now unable to live with Erasmus. She would have welcomed jealousy, recriminations, even punishment, but she cannot accept the monstrous hubris of "beyond good and evil." Her parting words to Erasmus are: "Even if you had shuddered at the emanations of the thousand fates that flow around my brow, I could have stayed with you—and perhaps our souls would have fused in the searing heat of unspeakable grief. But as it is, I am more horrified by the stony grimace of your wisdom than by all the masks and marvels of the world."

The message is unmistakable: moral relativism when carried to the ultimate leads to emotional paralysis and spiritual death.

A related idea is expressed in *Der letzte Brief eines Literaten* (written 1917, published 1932—untranslated). The unnamed protagonist, an extremely egocentric writer, elopes with his seriously ill fiancée, although he has been warned by her physician that she cannot survive the stresses of marriage. In the eyes of the young man his destructive action is justified not by his love for Maria but by his expectation that the tragic situation and the pain he expects to suffer from Maria's death can be utilized in writing a great literary work. His awakening conscience, however, makes him realize that he has committed an enormously evil act. He cannot undo the harm he has done—Maria is already dying—but he can permit his love for her to emerge fully, in this way adding happiness to her remaining days. It becomes impossible for him to live with what he has done, and he kills himself as she draws her last breath. Again, this is not a story written by a moral relativist.

Neither was *Casanova's Homecoming* written by one who was a moral relativist. It is not that the old adventurer in this tale is punished by a conscience that reproaches him for his life of immorality and depravity, but he loses everything he values most. In the end, old, repulsive, impoverished, dishonored, abandoned, he is despised by all including himself.

As to the question of free will, which is so central to Schnitzler's thinking, we find the clearest expression of Schnitzler's break with absolute determinism in his *Reflections and Aphorisms*, where he wrote:

> Can one really imagine a God who would simply be content to create the law of causality, whereupon—after the first impetus, with which he got the world started—all further events would occur as immutable and predetermined? No, He did not make it that easy for Himself. He placed into the universe an opponent worthy of Himself, free will—ready at any moment to combat causality, and to do so even when it believes itself that it is humbly submitting to an inscrutable decision.

Concerning Schnitzler's personal attitude toward religion, suffice it to state—on the basis of what he has written himself—that he never became religious in the common sense of the word. That is to say he remained highly skeptical, not to say hostile, toward "organized" religion, since he was fundamentally opposed to all intellectual rigorism and thus to anything constitutively dogmatic. Hence his aphorism, "If there is a God, then the way you worship him is sacrilege." Yet despite his basic skepticism, Schnitzler was not an atheist, as so many critics claim. Indeed, his very life and work substantiate his own observation: ". . . so far as my skepticism is concerned, there is in it so much reverence that it is probably closer to piety than what you call your faith."

Though he never accepted an anthropomorphic God-concept, he did recognize the existence of an abstract supreme power or principle. He attained a recognition of free will's role in human life as a potent counterforce to causality. There is no lack of thought-provoking comments on matters of religion in Schnitzler's writings, especially in *Reflections and Aphorisms*.

SOME DAY PEACE WILL RETURN:
NOTES ON WAR AND PEACE

Schnitzler's writings on war and peace consist of aphorisms and essays. With the exception of three items in his *Reflections and Aphorisms* and possibly a few others that may have appeared in the form of an occasional contribution to literary journals, they were not published during his lifetime. He never wrote a book or even a major essay on the subject of war, although the present notes could well have served as a basis for such a project. That he felt strongly about the matter is quite evident from the emotional intensity of his comments.

Was Schnitzler afraid to expose publicly his views on such a controversial issue? This is most unlikely. Many of his published works attest to the fact that he was not only extremely courageous in opposing social evils as he saw them but also undaunted by the sometimes distressing consequences of his unswerving honesty.

The thought that perhaps the task of producing a major sociophilosophical work may have transcended the skill or the intellectual capabilities of Schnitzler cannot be entertained seriously by anyone familiar with his study *The Mind in Words and Actions.*

Thus the only conclusion that remains is that Schnitzler did not *want* to write such a work. No one, of course, can say with certainty why he did not want to do so, and the following possibilities are offered merely as hypotheses.

Schnitzler was not a quixotic iconoclast. He did not believe the basic psychological structure of man could be changed. Not man but social institutions had to be improved. Premature attempts to effect such changes, however, are doomed to failure. Often the consequences of bad judgment in this respect are tragic. What an individual can accomplish if his time is ready for his message has been demonstrated, for instance, by Martin Luther and, in Schnitzler's time, by Émile Zola. Conversely, the fate of Woodrow Wilson may demonstrate the futility of trying for major reforms before their time has come.

Schnitzler knew this, and quite possibly he realized that the time was not yet ripe—that no nation was ready to pursue permanent peace at the price of even a slight sacrifice of national sovereignty.

Another possible reason for Schnitzler's failure to publish his thoughts on war and peace in expanded form comes to mind. With very few exceptions, his notes on this subject were written between 1914 and 1919, and publication during those years was out of the question. Then, soon after the end of World War I, the public was showered with pacifistic literature of all types. *Nie wieder Krieg!* (Never another war) was the dominant slogan of the day. With the countless condemnations of war—expressed in journals and newspapers, in novels, short stories, dramas, and poetry—a large number of proposals for the establishment of permanent peace were advanced. They ranged from lunatic schemes to brilliant ideas, and they poured out in endless succession. When the saturation point was reached, interest in the subject declined rapidly. The political chaos and the multiple economic crises became the prime concern for most Austrians and Germans. Most likely Schnitzler did not wish to add to the many publications on war and peace in the immediate postwar period. Even superior quality could hardly be expected to save it from being obscured by the quantity of other writings on this subject.

In 1939 the Bermann-Fischer publishing house, then in exile, published in Stockholm a selection from Arthur Schnitzler's notations on war and peace under the title *Über Krieg und Frieden*. The year of the pamphlet's appearance, however, was hardly propitious.

But what about the present? Are we now

ready to listen to reason, to consider seriously suggestions that could help us avert the ultimate catastrophe of thermonuclear war? Or is it too late once again?

Perhaps this work will be viewed with suspicion these days. In many minds pacifism has become synonymous with unworldliness, defeatism, cowardice, even treason.

It may be well to point out here that there are two fundamentally different types of pacifism. First, there is the one we may call didactic pacifism. Often based on religious, moral, or quasi-moral grounds, its proponents advocate refusal to participate in any military activity, even in self-defense against unprovoked attack. The second type may be termed humanistic pacifism. Dedicated to the proposition that human life is sacred and that, therefore, war is the most heinous crime imaginable, humanistic pacifism seeks to eliminate the causes of war, as a long-term goal. Its immediate aim is to make war impossible through the application of adequate safeguards to be agreed upon in negotiations and to be enforced by international organizations.

Schnitzler was a humanistic pacifist par excellence. His arguments are lucid and logical, his ideas worth thinking about, in spite or perhaps because of the fact that some of them may seem still "too far out" for immediate practical application.

The notes on war and peace illuminate Schnitzler's private thought processes more thoroughly than his other writings because they contain not only items that demonstrate his usual scientifically disciplined thinking but also a number of items presented in a nonscientific, less disciplined way. Schnitzler demonstrates his logical, scientific thinking as he develops his basic tenet: war is a form of criminally induced mass psychosis that can and must be made impossible. His nonscientific procedure, on the other hand, is revealed by the random order in which the notes are arranged, the repetition of statements, a number of obviously emotional remarks, and even some stylistic carelessness.

This makes *Some Day Peace Will Return: Notes on War and Peace* especially interesting, because it is in this collection of notes, alone among Schnitzler's writings, that we can observe his emotions guiding his pen. For once we are not confronted with a polished literary product, but may observe the feelings that motivated him. And the man who emerges is very different from the stereotyped descriptions of Schnitzler.

These notes were not written by a detached skeptic, not by a cynical behaviorist who sees human beings only as biological units. They were written by a man of deep compassion, by a writer who understood human weaknesses and who openly expressed his anger toward those who exploit such weaknesses, by a humanist who sadly recognizes his own helplessness to alter man's race toward self-annihilation.

In the many dramas and narratives that won worldwide fame for Schnitzler, overt preaching is carefully avoided. While he frequently presented ethical, social, and psychological problems and raised many questions, he carefully left any conclusions to the reader and proffered no solutions of his own. *Some Day Peace Will Return: Notes on War and Peace,* however, is a radical departure from this practice. Here he not only proclaims his attitude, but also proposes specific steps that he considered essential to eliminate war.

Unfortunately, almost all the political mistakes against which Schnitzler cautioned were subsequently made, and World War II became a reality. Even now measures for the preservation of world peace are being advocated publicly— measures quite in the spirit of those that Schnitzler recommended decades ago.

ABOUT THIS EDITION

The posthumous papers of Schnitzler are kept at Cambridge University in England. These papers, consisting of typed and handwritten manuscripts, drafts, notes, correspondence, and other papers, comprise about 265 numbered files. Complete microfilm copies are in the possession of Heinrich Schnitzler (Schnitzler's son and literary heir), the International Arthur Schnitzler Research Association, and several American and European universities.

Most of the writings that appear in this translation were discovered after Schnitzler's death in a separate file (Number 230), inscribed *"Und einmal wird der Friede wiederkommen"* ("Some Day Peace Will Return"). The typed pages in that file bear the notation *Abschriften* (copies), but the handwritten original is not there. Evidently there was some difficulty in making the transcription: some dates and words are followed by question marks, and on occasion the remark *unleserlich* (illegible) appears.

Only items 1 and 56–63 were located in a different file (Number 9), which contained miscellaneous aphorisms. Item 1 seems to have been written a full decade before World War I. It has been included here because it shows that Schnitzler's strong advocacy of peaceful coexistence and friendly exchange of ideas between the nations considerably antedated World War I. Items 56–63, even though undated, obviously do belong here. There is, moreover, some indication that they were originally part of File Number 230.

This edition is my translation of the German text as it appears in the previously mentioned *Aphorismen und Betrachtungen*. There are, however, a few differences in the present version. Two items that appear in the German edition, as well as parts of items 2, 5, 6, 24, and 25 are omitted, because they express—rather than generally applicable ideas—merely momentary or very personal reactions, impressions, and attitudes that digress from the primary topic. The entries in the present text are numbered and some are annotated.

The notes dated by Schnitzler are arranged in chronological order. They are followed by the undated material.

Where clarity demanded it, I have inserted bracketed words or phrases.

April 1971   ROBERT O. WEISS

Some Day Peace Will Return

1

1904[1]

PATRIOTIC. That silly clamor. "To feel patriotic." How does one serve his nation? How does one prove his love for it? By shouting: "I am a good German! We are the leading nation!"? By calling the other nations inferior? One is patriotic by endeavoring to perform at the very highest level possible within the limits of one's capabilities. Thus at the same time one benefits oneself and the nation to which one belongs. Only those who work are of importance to their nation; it can do without those who limit themselves to feeling patriotic.

As if it were still a question of superiority, as if it were a question of being more important than another nation and of being recognized or even of being feared as such by that other nation! It is exclusively a matter of perfecting one's abilities in a definite direction and of applying them with determination. Everything else is self-evident. The nations that are making progress are always distinctive by their habit of absorbing the achievements of other nations into the potentialities of their own development.

2

October 1914[2]

It is never premature to think of something and to formulate how one should like to react to it if one knows that it is inevitable, just as—in a certain sense—one can never start too soon to think about death.

Therefore, one should be prepared for peace as well as for war. It is perhaps just as difficult to accept peace in the right way, with the same dignified composure.

Let us not be confused, therefore, by the bitterness, the hate, the injustice (even the injustice probably has its reasons—and cannot be omitted from the psychological economy of warfare) with which the opponents now confront each other. Mankind knows from a thousand years of experience that there is no eternal hatred between countries, indeed that it will eventually abate, not only if vengeance has been fulfilled, but also if it has not been meted out.

Even if we ourselves should not live to see these passions assuaged, let us think of our sons and of our grandsons, for whose sake we are fighting the war, for whom we have to create peace. I may thus be permitted to say a few words at this early date, risking the possibility that they be lost in the din of battle, and that those who remain at home and only dimly perceive the threatening echo of the cannon, may not hear them, may reject them, may smile at them.

Some Day Peace Will Return 37

I never believed that the age of perpetual peace had arrived, and I do not believe that this monstrous war—were it to last seven or even thirty years—is the last one that civilized nations will conduct against one another.

But let us not forget in the depth of our souls that the enemies against whom our troops are fighting also have fathers and mothers, brothers and sisters, wives and children; that they all have a country, which almost all of them serve in the firm belief that its cause is just; and that even those have to serve their country who may doubt the justice of its cause. Let us remember that our enemies too, the foes of our soldiers, are sent into battle by their governments or their kings; that—willingly or unwillingly—they are obligated, indeed forced, to use their weapons against us, regardless of the degree of enthusiasm they have for that task. And let us keep in mind that later, therefore, once the war is over, we must not seek retribution for their actions from the citizens of a country that took up arms against us—not even in our feelings.

First, let us not believe everything that we are given to read, just as we desire that our enemies, for their part, do not believe blindly everything that is in their newspapers.
Furthermore, let us try to understand even the things that cannot be easily believed.
And finally, the most difficult task, let us at least resolve to forgive as soon as peace is made.

In the reconciliation, which to be sure will be

effected between the kings and governments with the usual display of emotionality, there must remain no sediment of hatred among the peoples—no matter how it all ends.

There are neutral states, so-called neutral states that is, and among these there may be one or another that will yet take sides in this monstrous war, though at this moment we cannot tell which side they may favor. It is just as possible that—before this war is over—our soldiers will fight side by side with those who are still neutral as it is that they will fight against them. And those soldiers of the country that is neutral now have no idea at this moment whether or not they may be obligated tomorrow to hate mortally our soldiers or love them fraternally. It is their government that will dictate that to them. But so tremendous is the power of politics, so much more tremendous at least in its practical effects than national and other sympathies and antipathies, that we can already state that the soldiers of this now still neutral country, all of them, will be either our faithful comrades in arms or our mortal enemies. Not one among those hundreds of thousands will be guided by his personal feelings and decide for or against us in opposition to his government. If, however, one of these soldiers obligated to fight should inwardly arrive at a conclusion other than that of his government or his king, and should he act in accordance with that conclusion—which may possibly be a much more sensible one than that at which his king has arrived—he will probably have to pay for that action with his life.

As depressing as this consideration may appear in a higher sense, it offers a certain consolation for the future. It tells us this: as soon as the governments so desire, peace will be here. Indeed, as terrible, as shaming as the thought is, we all know that the authoritative command of one person, even if it originates out of a momentary whim, is quite sufficient to restrain a hate-filled crowd of people that, ready to attack, lurks across from an opposing crowd. We know that such a command of one man would suffice to force a hundred thousand swords back into their scabbards, to deactivate the deadly projectiles in a hundred thousand gunbarrels and cannon muzzles. And after another moment, a sigh of relief, of release, would go through all of this enormous accumulation of men that was ready a second ago—either unthinkingly or enthusiastically—to cause or to suffer destruction. And those who are able to make an accounting in their own minds would realize in a flash of enlightenment: "We don't want to kill at all, we don't want to bleed to death at all! We want to breathe, live, eat our daily bread, have a bit of land to live on, and work." At that great moment, with peace spreading over the land, all of them would know that they never did want anything else—even those who a minute ago were aiming at the hearts of their enemies and who were ready to die for their country.

Not the most shocking but perhaps the most saddening fact is that this time the intellectuals, who, we had hoped, would make it possible for us to extend our hands to them across the abyss of this war, are failing us almost entirely, that they either will not or cannot see the real facts.

Ridiculous, even shameful, seems to me the despondency of some [writers and] artists who suddenly feel superfluous because there is now no demand for their work. The military certainly did not feel superfluous for half a century during which we did not seem to need them, and they were quite right not to feel so. And neither have the [writers and] artists become superfluous now. They should continue to prepare silently and to be always in readiness. Peace may break out at any moment. Woe to you if you are not prepared.

What does it mean to be ripe for one's time? To give to it one's all and yet preserve one's integrity in it.

One sees so many these days who spend themselves, squander their strength—in a feverish and mostly futile activity—strength they could make fruitful use of not only for their own benefit and for that of their families but also, in a broader sense, for that of their country, though perhaps in ways that are not so obvious.

3

November 1914

This war is unprecedented for the heroism with which it is being fought by the armies, and for the malice with which it is being waged by the countries, especially by some governments, and by the journalists.

The respect of the armies for each other is

growing; the bitterness between the nations is increasing.

One can readily imagine that someday (as is already happening in isolated instances) the opposing troops will greet each other with affection and enthusiasm, that the officers will salute each other respectfully, and that in indifference to all this, far behind them, the diplomats and citizens will continue to revile each other as usual.

4

December 1914

No reprisals! One should not put oneself in the wrong. Again and again it is the innocent upon whom the blows fall. And afterward, naturally, it will not be possible to discern exactly who started it all. It would be of inestimable value for the future peace negotiations and especially for the subsequent relations between the countries if the Germans and Austrians were to maintain their composed and civilized deportment toward those subjects of enemy countries who happen to live in their midst.

5
December 1914

The most important moral of this war: the complete collapse of the claim that ethnic and religious differences constitute a cause of war.

A power game between the nations, that is the crucial factor here. The complete victory of absolutism.

It looks, for instance, as if the Romanians as well as the Italians could intervene, or could have intervened, just as easily on the side of Germany as on the side of her enemies—that it has always been left only to the discretion, to the whim, at the very best to the conviction, of a single individual who was given power, to bring about the decisions as to which side the nations would align themselves with. Even republics are ruled in an absolutistic manner. What will be at issue is to make that impossible.

The old demand: the people have to decide about war and peace.

An apparent impossibility.

But really only seemingly so.

Defensive war, of course, cannot be eliminated.

It is the war of aggression that is crucial.

It will not do, however, on the one hand to praise war as a grandiose, a colossal, and in a certain sense a divine, necessity that causes everything noble as well as everything evil in man to attain magnificent heights; to declare that a long peace renders nations sluggish and cowardly; to claim that war cleanses and purifies—and on the other hand to curse those who unleash the war and to hold them responsible for the fact that they were handily available at the proper time, so to speak, for the divine necessity.

6

January 1915

Many feuilletonists claim that after this war humanity will somehow be cleansed and purified.

The reasons for this assumption are not clear: none of the wars thus far waged in the world has produced this result.

Political reaction is almost invariably the consequence of victorious wars; revolution, the consequence of lost ones. Both consequences are, as it were, conditions of exhaustion.

Naturally, every event has the power to bring out, in some people with a tendency in that direction, great and noble qualities that otherwise would have had no chance to develop.

The same, however, goes for bad qualities.

Besides, one would have to agree on the way of looking at the problem. Some actions look like heroic acts, but one should not overlook the fact that—precisely in times of war—situations very frequently occur in which bravery is the surest way of escaping danger.

It is easily conceivable, for instance, that the same young man who tramples defenseless children and women to death during a fire in order to get outside, will, as an officer, lead men in an attack with a total contempt of death.

Moreover, one must have time to develop his great qualities. Who will be the purified? Those who have lost a leg or an eye? The parents who have lost a child, the woman who has lost her husband? The people who perished? The people who made millions from defense contracts? The diplomats who planned the war? The monarchs, victorious or defeated? The journalists who stayed at home? Those who will be purified—I venture to suspect—have already been so before.

7
January 1915

"A monarch almost never wants war. Everyone must be forced into war." (The foregoing is a remark of Professor Redlich).[3] In his official position a monarch is a puppet, unless he is a genius like Friedrich or Napoleon. Outside of it, he is a human being like everybody else. Tragic conflicts arise from this situation.

8
January 1915

An ethnopsychological fact: Under reigns of long duration, individual subjects somehow adapt themselves outwardly and inwardly to the type of their monarch. The weaker the individual, and the closer he stands to the monarch socially or just ideologically, the more clearly the similarity will emerge.

(*A remark made by Professor Redlich, M.P., in a conversation.*)

9
January 1915

Heroism as a virtue of circumstances. The same person who might crush a child under foot during a sudden conflagration would lead his troops into the enemy's fire.

Heroism as a means of keeping alive.

Cowardice under control.

10
January 1915

World history is a conspiracy of the diplomats against common sense.

11
January 1915

Which then is the characteristic feature of war? Death? Everybody is subject to that experience, including those who have never been in a war. Heroism? For that, human civilization holds innumerable better opportunities. Suffering? Poverty? Brutality? In all their diverse manifestations? In this respect the yield of war exceeds only quantitatively that of peaceful epochs.

The only thing specific to war is the wound, the senseless physical wound, and hostility, the senseless hostility, i.e., the hostility between human beings who, as individuals, might be facing each other without hate, perhaps even with love.

12
January 1915

The conspiracy of the peoples against the mighty is an occasional occurrence; the conspiracy of the mighty against the peoples is the normal condition of the world. Even during a bloody war the king feels—although sometimes unconsciously—closer and more related to the other king, the king with whom he is at war, than to his equerry, to his prime minister, or even to his adjutant.

13
February 1915

How do wars become possible?

(1) By the knavery of the powerful, (2) by the stupidity of diplomats, and (3) by the lack of imagination on the part of the peoples.

That lack is reinforced through flight into the abstract—customary in history and politics.

Pluralization per se has the mysterious power magically to transform the concrete into the abstract.

A thousand wounded soldiers appear by no

means so terrible to one's imagination as one wounded soldier. They represent not a thousand times one, nor one wounded soldier, nor a fraction of one, but actually something qualitatively different.

It is in the interest of the state to support this faulty thinking, not to consider the individual. The state itself, after all, shows the way by setting a bad example.

The inability of people, even of those with rich imagination, to fully imagine anything is extraordinary and always surprising. This lack of imagination is explicable only as an internal defense mechanism, gradually developed in the course of time, against the ghastliness of a world that cannot be borne by the human senses. If one could imagine death, then life would be unbearable, in a manner of speaking. And just as he does not imagine death, man does not ever really imagine the end of anything, separation and sorrow. That which he is accustomed to call "imagination" is memory, and actually not even memory of facts but memory of words or images. Only the fact that everything that happens is a memory the very next moment makes our life possible at all. Some of what we call insanity is undoubtedly nothing but a capacity—caused by an innate or acquired intensity of feeling—to hold on to the moment, to prevent it from immediately becoming a memory. And imagination in its ultimate form is nothing more than the holding on to a heightened moment—in other words, experiencing in the present a past experience, sometimes even one in the future. If this ability were general, or if it operated uninterruptedly in certain people, the concept of time customary in social interaction (but by no means the philosophical concept of time) would thereby be eliminated.

But just as the total supremacy of imagination would ultimately mean insanity, so a complete lack of imagination means feeblemindedness. And this feeblemindedness (precisely in the pathological meaning of the word) is that mental state of mankind, which is prevalent not only among the masses but even among those people who—by endowment, vocation, and personal development—could be considered as obligated to observe with a wide-awake consciousness, the history of mankind or even to influence it.

14

February 1915

Strange as it sounds, at the future peace congress it should not be permitted to speak of politics in a retrospective sense. The question of guilt must not be brought up—for how far would one have to trace back history in order to arrive at a completely just verdict? It would of course be shortsighted to speak only of the most recent causes of the war. And yet one would get nowhere if one were to attempt to uncover one cause after another in an unrelenting search for the true source of the evil. There is no remedy but a complete amnesty that includes the most recent past. One would have to make a serious attempt to usher in a new epoch. And just as in civil life we must not hold up to a convicted transgressor his past after he has served his sentence, it should not be permitted on the politico-historical scene to reproach the culprit with his guilt, whether it was atoned for or not.

We shall find no country that was entirely wrong, none that was entirely right. On the whole, one can probably only say that the party that was attacked and that also had the most to lose by war, was probably less guilty and less to blame than those who attacked and whose risk had been a smaller one.

But there is a difference between threat, aggression, and surprise attack—and there is a difference between vigilance, defense, and preventive war.

Since there are transitional situations here where not only judgment but also sentiment are necessarily involved, it will not be possible to pronounce a decision that is entirely incontestable in the logical, political, and historical sense.[4]

15

March 1915

Necessity to fight two dogmas:

(1) The dogma of the fated necessity of war.

(2) The dogma of the purifying effect of war.

Difficulties. We are confronted by the mental inertia of people, the tradition of a thousand years, alleged lessons of history, the organization of the world as it appears to us, and the universally human attributes of stupidity and lack of imagination.

The dangerous nature of the latter is underestimated.

The mighty make it their business to support this characteristic.

Instead of images, rhetoric is given to people.

Instead of the multitudinous concrete, they are given abstracts.

It is an old habit of human beings to escape from multiple reality so totally unbearable and probably also incomprehensible into the coolness of the conceptual. That is not always an elevation into the symbolic, but a flight into the abstract.

It is the same old political trick of disregarding the individual and reckoning only with the masses—in contrast to the artist, who resolves the mass into individuals.

This error, rather this deliberate deception, is to be dispelled—an undertaking that can succeed only if the rational elements of all countries are in agreement among themselves, i.e., when the power of rational people has become so great that it can prevail over the power of the stupid, the scoundrels, the mighty. The mighty are by no means necessarily either one or the other—they often suffer only from inherited defects or from those of their métier.

16

May 1915

A tremendous disproportion exists between the sensation that motivates the soldier and the way by which he must, perforce, express it. He loads a rifle, fires it, and certainly has no conscious awareness that he is not only annihilating a human life (or, as an artillery man, a hundred lives) but also destroying dozens of relationships, etc. He has in any case a feeling closer to being engaged in a sport than to being involved in a human, let alone a philosophical, matter. Here, too, as in everything that is even remotely connected with politics, the aim is to keep people in a state of ignorance. The whole of world history is but an intrigue of the powerful directed against the consciousness and the imagination of the individual or, rather, of the masses.

17

May 1915

War and criticism.

The attitude of the poets[5] toward the war has been discussed often enough.

But those who most deserve to be viewed with misgivings—the critics—come off best, as usual.

Among the poets, at least some are silent; among the critics, none.

They have something to say about this world

war, and also about the relation of the poets to the world war.

Ex officio, they watch carefully how the poets conduct themselves with respect to the war and feel they have to issue statements.

They find it remarkable that some poets create and that others remain silent. Even the silence does not cause them to shut up—no, they criticize even the silence. Sometimes they praise it, and in the process they insinuate that the poet, who is not nearly so clever, so politically enlightened, and so generally superior as the critic, could probably do nothing better.

Neither is the private life of the poet immune to their criticism. Richard Dehmel[6] goes to the frontlines, he is photographed, he writes a letter to his children, and it is published. One may consider that more or less tasteful. (I personally should have no objection to that.) The critic finds fault with it. In the photographs and in the published letter he sees a vanity that is not worthy of the time, not worthy of the poet. For the critic is never vain, he never has himself photographed, and he always publishes only articles by which he advances the cause of mankind.

All right. The poet writes a letter to his children. At any rate, it is interesting enough, even if a little vanity is involved. But what Schmock[7] has to say on the subject of Mr. Dehmel's letter to his children is totally uninteresting.

Somewhere I also read that Dehmel went to war only because spiritually he was finished as a poet and needed new material for his work. Thus he is being annotated while still alive and exposed not only to rifle bullets and shrapnel but to the stink bombs of the critics as well. And they will continue flying through the world, even when the cannon are silent.

What a magnificent opportunity to apply a new criterion to the works of the poets and their literary creations: the war and the heroes who are fighting out there. Already the critics are out to determine which works and which poets have been swept away forever by the hurricane of this great time, and they flatter themselves with the illusion that they are engaged in combat and contributing to the purification.

The critics revile also the people who sit at home and compose poems. But the critics are not in the trenches either; they sit at home while they criticize the people who compose poems and those who compose none. The critics—they are the people whose activities are never put to an end. They are as troublesome and as superfluous, as mendacious and as insolent in wartime as they were in peacetime. Nothing is swept away. Peace will come. On this subject, too, the poets will be heard, and others will be silent. The critics will watch and take offense. Such is their trade.

18

1915

War atrocity: a defenseless wounded man was blinded and mutilated on the battlefield—by an enemy, of course.

I can tell a worse tale. A dozen soldiers were

sitting in a trench as a shrapnel struck. One was blinded, another had his abdomen slit open, the third had his larynx shredded, the entire face of the fourth was torn off, the fifth had both arms and a leg shattered, and so forth. Those who were not immediately killed lay there for hours suffering thirst, torments, hellish pain, the fear of death. They too had been defenseless, completely defenseless. There was no possibility of defending themselves against the shrapnel. Also, they could not run off, for had they done so, they would have been shot for cowardice, according to law. The obligation to defend their country had rendered them defenseless.

19

1915

Childishly we bewail the misfortune of those who die during the war, because they will never know its outcome. As if anyone could live to see the outcome! Did the people in 1873 suspect that what they were witnessing was not yet the end of the war of 1870–1871? One is reminded of the proposal of an alderman who wanted to have some change carried out only when all old people had died.

The thesis of Clausewitz that war is nothing but politics by different means is witty, therefore half-true, therefore dangerous, therefore nonsense.[8]

So also is the dictum that war is a necessity

and that therefore one must not oppose it. Plague and cholera too are "necessities." Only the fact that we do oppose such alleged necessities makes us really human beings. And, in any case, defending oneself is also a necessity. If we do not believe in free will, the world is clearly nonsensical. And we have every reason to believe in free will. Since free will was capable of creating the world, it cannot have vanished from the world.[9]

The only indubitable possession of man is his life. All his other possessions—money, fame, power—are, at least at times, tenuous possessions in one respect or the other. Compulsory military service, however, is the most monstrous violation of the one indubitable possession of man.[10] Moreover it is imposed for the benefit of very dubious ideas—in general as well as in particular—such as dynasty, country, state.

20

1915

The sense of solidarity of those in power, even when they are at war with each other, is more deeply rooted than the sense of solidarity that the peoples feel for each other, even when they live in peace with each other.

Absolutism is a tradition; it is as ancient as world history. One could even say it is an idea, an innate idea, grounded in the most genuine instincts of mankind. (Every human being is a priori an absolutist where his own affairs are concerned—simply by being an egoist, and having to be one.) But wherever in the world human beings embody or personify this idea of absolutism, as kings as well as presidents do, then they clasp hands fraternally across centuries and across national borders.

Conversely, the democratic idea is young, no older than the modern state which actually does not yet exist and which we are only now striving to develop. The democracy of classical antiquity has hardly anything to do with ours because the economic, social, and religious conditions at that time were completely different. Modern democracy has hardly been in existence longer than since 1848. One must not even trace it back to the French Revolution.

In spite of these facts, or rather because of them, those in power distrust each other also in times of peace, even in times of existing alliances, and the peoples feel a certain shy, awkward tenderness for each other, even when they are forced to mount armed attacks against each other.

On the fertile ground of these peculiar relationships diplomacy originated. Such contradictions are always fertile ground for the idle talkers and the meddlers.

21

1915[11]

In the near future those with common sense should use it to appropriate the power instead of being satisfied with basking in their righteousness and wisdom. Once they are in power, there is no longer anything to prevent them from putting that righteousness and wisdom to full use. Yes, only then will those beautiful qualities become meaningful. Until such time they will almost be harmful.

22 •

March 1916

Once the discussion on the preconditions for world peace can be opened seriously, all participants, as well as all those who speak on this question at all, should obligate themselves to refrain from raising certain points, the discussion of which would be completely hopeless, would only constitute a loss of time as well as a waste of intellectual and emotional strength, and indeed, through the unleashing of passionate arguments would inevitably make the entire discussion unpleasant, if not futile.

These topics then would have to be excluded:

(1) The guilt question as it pertains to all preceding wars and particularly with respect to the most recent war. It should be assumed as an established fact that all nations are to blame for this war, that no one nation wanted it. It was wanted by no one people but only by an infinitesimal number of individuals.

(2) The discussion of individual war atrocities. Here, too, it appears useless to differen-

tiate. It remains the same enormity whether so-called civilians, women, and children are killed and maimed from the air, whether one plans to condemn these civilians to death by starvation, or whether young men and older men (just as disinterested and just as innocent as the civilians and—whether or not they are clearly aware of that fact—forced into war service) are killed or crippled by murderous weapons. Moreover, villainy and heroism, treason and patriotism, are so close to one another in times of war that in the individual case a differential diagnosis by an impartial judge can only seldom be made and that the decision must be left to merely opportunistic considerations. Everything, absolutely everything, that war brings in its wake is equally gruesome in its senselessness, in its brutality.

(3) In future discussions, considerations, and proposals, the possibility that mankind as a whole could become better and wiser in the foreseeable future should not be considered at all. We should, rather, again and again proceed from the conviction that human beings will remain feeble-thinking, suggestible creatures. Nevertheless, even in their cowardice they are capable of every kind of so-called heroism.

So little should one believe in an improvement of human beings that one can instead postulate the following as an immutable axiom: So long as there is on this earth a single person who, without any perceptible danger to himself, sees a possibility of obtaining an advantage for himself, even at the price of a hundred thousand corpses and cripples, and so long as this same person possesses the power and influence to bring about a war, just so long mankind must not consider itself safe from the danger of war. Man is the most pitiless being in all creation. In general, his compassion does not extend beyond the sorrow that his senses can perceive. And the profound anecdote about the man sitting peacefully in his room having only to press a button to have a wish fulfilled at the trifling price of a mandarin's head, which is cut off in China at the same moment—this anecdote applies not only to defense contractors and diplomats, to kings and generals, but to all of us. If the man in the room with his finger on the button knew, or if he could even imagine that he himself in turn was the mandarin to someone else, then perhaps he would think twice about pressing the button.

What, then, is the problem? To remold the structure of government in such a way that the very existence of such an individual (to whom war can give an advantage and who also has the power to unleash it) becomes absolutely impossible.

The difficulties of such reorganization are, of course, enormous and can be overcome only though an organization extending over the whole inhabited earth, an organization of all those people to whom war can bring only disadvantages. And since they are undoubtedly in the majority, by a hundred thousand or a million times, one should think that the difficulties of founding such an organization should not be insuperable after all, considering the enormous advantage it would bring to the overwhelming majority of mankind. All conferences held in the individual countries for the attainment of world peace would have to have as a prerequisite the creation of such an international and supranational organization. On the other hand, the federation of the component parts—at first deliberating separately in their individual countries—would at a certain moment have to come into being automatically.

These tendencies were foreshadowed in international social democracy even prior to this war. In general, its so-called failure can be explained by the fact that—as things stand today—social democracy, indeed democracy in general, is hardly even in its infancy as compared to absolutism. (The term democracy does not at all mean government by the people but, rather, a form of government operated for the benefit of, and in accordance with, the wishes of the people.)

To create that organization is the task and the duty of all rational persons. I am not saying "of all friends of the human race!" One does not have to love the human race to rebel against the idea that the fate of millions is entrusted to the hands of a few individuals who, unfortunately, are only seemingly responsible people. It is necessary that people find the way to each other in the spirit of justice, liberty, and humanity, which, combined, we might call the concept of divine reason.

Therefore, world peace, in this context, has nothing whatever to do with love of mankind. It is almost sufficient that everyone love himself, his relatives, his native country (we deliberately avoid here the word fatherland) in order to realize that world peace is worth the most intensive effort.

Naturally, the chances for success of the world-peace idea will the more increase as less work and energy will have to be expended on arguments or fights with the opponents of this world-peace idea. Hence their subterfuges and excuses, their credulity, and their platitudes, would have to be refuted decisively before the beginning of the positive phase of the work. It is quite obvious that the friends of world peace cannot forge ahead with their work so long as there are not only people who look upon war as something rooted in the order of the universe, as something that can never be eliminated, but also those who praise war as something exalted, something beautiful, something beneficial to the development of mankind as a whole. These people would have to be silenced as completely and permanently as, for example, lunatics who consider the plague as something rooted in the order of the universe, as something generally beneficial to mankind, and who therefore would refuse to collaborate in the decontamination of regions infested by the plague, to stamp out the focuses of the plague—or who would even, from some perverted aesthetic enjoyment, distribute cultures of the plague bacillus all over the world. This comparison seems to be exaggerated and somehow offensive. The fact that people could see it that way merely constitutes further proof that the rhetoric of the splendor and the purifying power of war still has something like the force of a dogma.

So that this organization may become a real-

ity, it is necessary not only to fight the enemies of the peace idea but above all to get to know them. These enemies are:
(1) The philosophers of war (war is politics conducted by different means).
(2) The fatalists (it has always been this way, therefore it must always continue in this way).
(3) The snobs (war, courage, adventure, etc., are somehow elegant).
(4) The phasemongers (those who speak of the purifying effect of war).

Let us assume a few people really become morally better through their personal wartime experiences and that a few neurasthenics are even cured through them. That seems to be somewhat too high a price to pay for the sacrifices imposed on all the others.

They say a nation attains its highest potential only after a war. This is not true. People in general have certainly not become better or more talented after a war. There are only the infinite number of those who are worse off economically and a few who are better off economically.

Furthermore, to prove the opposite is inherently impossible.

Who can prove to me that all nations would not be better off without war?

Necessary also is the fight against that kind of literature that exalts war. Other fields of endeavor offer the opportunity of attaining all that is praiseworthy in war, all that deserves glorification: courage, self-sacrifice, adventure, etc.

It is quite characteristic that those very men who talked about the great era, who celebrated specific exploits, who intentionally brought about the war, now long for its end.

Now all of you bewail in desperation the insanity of war. Well, do not all of you, or almost all of you, share in the guilt? By having looked in peacetime upon war—which today you consider insanity—as something quite rational, by having talked about it as if it were something rational? Did you not place war within the economy of our thinking, not among the insane and the criminal types of action but among the just and rational ones? You really did speak of war as of politics continued by different means; as of something that had as legitimate a right to existence as negotiations—even as peace itself. You spoke of it as something that could be considered permissible even by decent people of sound mind—often enough, as a matter of fact, as something exalted or even something inevitable.

And you who went cheering to the battlefield and wrote enthusiastic letters home—you who today, if you have not been killed in the meantime or become crippled or insane, long for the end and shout your disgust to the world, your horror, your boundless anger at the senseless slaughter of human beings—did you really not know at that time, when you went to the battlefield so enthusiastically, what war was? Did you not know that the word war, like a transparent and fragile bowl, contains all those other words —murder, mutilation, robbery, pillage, pestilence, blindness, lice, poisoning, being burned alive, suffocation, dying of thirst, as well as a hundred more of the like—that now suddenly, since the bowl is finally broken, fly through the air like evil insects, darkening the atmosphere?

And all of you who are now about to sigh and moan and curse and look for the guilty ones and want to hang the culprits—are you not all guilty since, after all, you did base your entire existence, the education of your children, your everyday life, your whole philosophy on the premise that war was something permissible, indeed something rational, indeed something necessary; that—you can no longer believe it today, yet it is true, and you could have heard and read it a thousand times—it was even something beautiful, something exalted and purifying. Did you not make of the history of the world a history of battles, of combat, rather than a history of the human spirit?

And your rulers, each of whom would now like to disclaim responsibility for even the slightest part of the blame for this horror—do they not all, nevertheless, go about in the vestments of war instead of in civilian dress? And did they not do so even in times of deepest peace?

And all the career officers, who now also want the killing to be stopped—did they not build their lives upon the premise that every now and then such a killing would be ordered? Indeed, did they not actually long for it—not, as one might think, for the sake of their country, but for the benefit of their careers, from thirst for adventure, from boredom?

And the diplomats—each of whom would now like to appear innocent—did they not time and again deliberate whether, in this case or that, the nation's honor or the nation's profitable trade could be maintained or continued through peaceful negotiations or whether it might not be essential to reach for the sword for reasons of prestige, territorial gain, or of more profitable trade? Even the [international] courts of arbitration of which they spoke were not to decide and pronounce judgments. Rather, it was to be left to the discretion of a nation, a people, a state, whether they would be willing to submit to the decision of such an arbitration court.

If all this was hitherto assumed to be the "natural course of the world," if all this was sensible and worthy of serious thought, in short, if war was something rational so long as it was only a possibility—how do they dare see it as senseless and insane now that it is reality?

23

You wish to render war more humane?

To do so, one would have first to make human beings more humane. And that seems impossible.

Not cruelty, which, after all, appears only as an acute illness, as it were, but indifference is the terrible evil, because it is the more dangerous and more inconquerable of the two. For, basically, we are all more or less indifferent. This indifference probably developed during man's struggle for survival since the ability to go on living, was made possible only through such indifference. Those in the true sense of the word compassionate (not the sentimentalists) had to die out. In reality, we are all without compassion. What do we care about the hundred thousand who are killed by an earthquake in Australia? What do we care about twenty thousand enemies killed? What—if we are to be quite honest—do we care about ten thousand fallen countrymen of ours, countrymen whom we do not know, who mean nothing to us? The range of our hearts' vision is barely ten feet. Of course, we grieve for our son, our brother, our nephew, our friend, even perhaps for just an acquaintance of ours—but does our heart beat faster when we see the name of Mr. X from Schärding[12] on the list of the critically wounded? To be sure, the cripple who just limped by, or the blinded veteran who is just being led by— they might bring tears to our eyes. But do we cry a thousand times as much when we read about a thousand cripples? No, not even as much as we cried at the sight of that one cripple.

We totally lack the gift of imagination. We come closer to possessing fantasy. Fantasy is without discipline and approaches the realm of the irrational; therefore, we can cope with it. We have the right not to believe in its images. But we fend off the concrete visions of our imagination, probably in order to be able to go on living at all. How many were killed yesterday? Forty thousand. Horrible! On the following day, a correction appears: there were forty-one thousand. Do our hearts beat harder because of those additional thousand? And herein lies a partial explanation of why nothing is done, why —in a higher sense—nothing can be done to change the world fundamentally. For I speak only of those who have some kind of conscience, who are not completely devoid of compassion, even of those who have the honest will to change the world. These people—there can be no doubt about it—suffer also from the general misery and horror, quite apart from that which happens to each one individually. But how indistinct, how vague, how weak beyond words is this compassion. What we must remember now, however, is that a tremendous majority of mankind is virtually insensitive so far as the weal and woe of all is concerned, that by far the greatest number of human beings are prepared at any moment to permit—for the sake of honor, for fame, for advancement of their career, for a decoration, for an opportunity to make money— thousands, even hundreds of thousands, of people to perish in the most pitiful manner, as long as they themselves are not among the victims. Actually, some of them accept even this risk, being supported in such ventures precisely by that lack of the gift of imagination.

24

March 1916

Concerning Rolland's collected essays *Au-dessus de la mêlée*.[13]

I find they contain the strongest justification for my demand that those who intend to debate the conditions and possibilities of a future world peace must not engage in further discussions about the past, and especially not about the causes of this war.[14]

25
1916

Which heroic death is the more enviable one? Death by a well-aimed bullet or a stray bullet? Death through typhus or a grenade? The death of the youth who has his life still ahead of him or that of a father who leaves behind children unprovided for?

26
1916

The only positive factor that is cited again and again as evidence that we are living in a great era is the fact that a number of persons are enabled to let certain qualities shine forth, which we should not have learned of in normal times or which would not have developed at all in such times, i.e., bravery and willingness to make sacrifices. If we now consider that the same applies also to the bad qualities, not to mention all the other evils of war, then we must say that the, at best, aesthetic pleasure of seeing a journeyman tailor act as a hero is purchased at rather too high a price. How very peculiar that it is just this, as it were, esthetic view of the war that is expressed by those people who habitually display a tremendous contempt for aestheticism.

27

1916

The argument that there will always be wars because human beings will not change within the foreseeable future is untenable. One could have advanced the same argument with reference to the Inquisition, the burning of witches, the practice of torture, and it is quite beyond doubt that human beings as such are no better today than they were hundreds of years ago. The essential thing, however, is not that human beings are brutal, cruel, envious, vengeful, but that they are weak, in the sense that they can so easily be influenced. This is also the only way to understand what many superficial observers consider the purifying effect of war, namely the incidents of self-sacrifice, bravery, etc. (More about this elsewhere in these notes.)[15] It is not the people that must be improved, but the organizations. The important goal for these organizations is not that of achieving solidarity or fraternization—at least not in a sentimental sense—but only that of showing very clearly just what it is that is practical or perhaps even advantageous for the individual. A possible [peace] movement must start with this idea.

28

1916

The enemies:
  (1) The dogmatists who proclaim the war as a fated necessity.
      ORIGIN: intellectual inertia.
  (2) The philosophers. Their motto: War is politics by different means.
      SUBDIVISIONS: idle talkers, feuilletonists, literary hacks.
      ORIGIN: superficiality, stupidity, pomposity.
  (3) The snobs, for whom war represents something essentially reactionary, something elegant, something similar to being pious and monarchistic.
      ORIGIN: cowardice, the need to find shelter.

29

1916

An international law? Why don't we bury that dream.
And let us dream that dream again when a people's law we have.
For in the craze of war both laws are only dreams.
Now ours is the choice: traitors or slaves to be.

Your choice then take—which do you want to be![16]

30

1916

War has never actually been waged for an idea; neither for a national nor for a religious one. (That can be proved not only with regard to this war.) Ideas are always used as a pretence—they are, so to speak, carried ahead as a banner, as the flags of the soul. Naturally, any phrase can be elevated to the status of an idea. This is one of the principal tasks of the politician—who in turn restores the balance by making a phrase of every idea.

31

1917

The hate against the people who enrich themselves through war and derive their livelihood from it has permitted the aversion against those who base their livelihoods upon the possibility, the expectation, the continuous taking into account the possibility of war—the military and the diplomats—to recede all too far into the background. It is they who always poison peace by thoughts of war.

32

1917

I knew a lady who switched her allegiance from the Central Powers to the Entente because a gentleman at the next table was smoking, and she had once heard that Englishmen never smoke in the presence of ladies.

33

1918

It is not the settlement of national boundaries that matters, but rather that of bringing about a time when it will be a matter of complete indifference just where the borders are, a time when borders will have merely administrative significance—just as, for example, a boundary between two Italian cities today that were at war with each other centuries ago no longer means that the people of these cities can hate and kill each other and that they sometimes even imagine they have to do so.

34

1919

Never has war been waged for the sake of an idea. Never has it been a matter of anything but a struggle for power. But ideas—whether believed or not—have always been indispensable as pretexts.

The claim that the Thirty Years' War was a religious war is a historical falsification. The proof to the contrary is the fact that just a few years after its beginning Protestants were fighting in the emperor's army and Catholics were fighting on the side of his adversaries. And in the second half of the war the ratio was virtually reversed.

Not only can it be proved that the ideas for the sake of which wars have been waged were fraudulently presented to the peoples or the armies concerned, but it can also be proved that the leaders, those who themselves unleashed the wars, disbelieved in the ideas which they claimed they were fighting for, or that they were monomaniacs.

Naturally, the art of voluntarily blacking out selected areas of one's own soul, an art developed to a high degree of perfection in politicians, plays here an important part.

35
1919

They write and act not just as if Germany had plotted this war, but as if Germany had actually invented war.

Their ignorance of history comes in handy to them.

Nevertheless, it can hardly be unknown to

even the most ignorant person that wars have
been waged as long as the world has existed,
and—this is the essential thing—that war was
always taken into account as a possibility, if
not as a necessity. To start or even to declare a
war was never considered a monstrous villainy
as such (even though it probably always was
that). Martial, combative, and other words with
similar meanings were by no means considered
to be derogatory (even though they should perhaps always have been considered such).

But let us rejoice, nevertheless, that for the
time being (it will probably not last long) the
overwhelming majority of mankind seems to
have arrived at the proper concept, ethically, of
the nature of war and, psychologically, of the
nature of heroism. By no means did this concept
exist in the year 1914.[17]

36

Nothing is more disgraceful for the nation, for
the people, for the citizen, than the so-called
blue books and similar documents. Only when
the gravest decisions have been made do we
learn that conversations and consultations
among a very small number of persons have been
decisive—and that they have been conducted by
nonentities, by idle persons, by even important
persons for all I care, but at any rate fallible
ones.

Later on, of course, they claim everything was

historical necessity. But even a historical necessity has its individual causes, and we must remember that in the world of ideas nothing has, as it were, a brighter future than the political event that becomes a fact of universal historical significance.

Even the so-called historical necessity is nothing but the law of causality which is equally valid for the smallest and the largest. We must consider either everything or nothing as inescapable, as necessary. If we believe that the will of the individual is sufficiently powerful to deflect the sequence of necessities, then we have the right to seek this will everywhere—in the private life of the individual as well as in the course of the events for which universal historical significance is claimed.

37

Anecdotes are repeatedly told about enemies confronting each other in the trenches who signal each other during breaks in firing, meet in no-man's-land, exchange cigarettes and food, shake hands—once, two of them are said to have embraced each other, weeping—and then return to their trenches to shoot each other without hatred. They have met face to face.

Behind them is the artillery. The cannons are fired at unknown, invisible people, into a void, as it were, at an undifferentiated mass, without hatred.

Behind them, in turn, are the staffs in the headquarters. To them, the entire matter is primarily a mathematical problem. The concept of the individual human being fades more and more; it is a game with figures that just happen to be human beings. Here, again, there is no hatred between man and man.

Still farther behind them are the diplomats. Here deals are made in money, power, fame, careers. Rarely is there among them a statesman who has farsightedness. Even here there is no hatred. Still farther to the rear are the governments and the royal courts. Here they are related to each other by marriage. The day before yesterday they embraced each other. There were toasts, assurances of friendship. Only yesterday they promised and implored each other to do everything for the preservation of the peace. And today there should be hate? It is only jealousy. Jealousy that was there the day before yesterday, and yesterday—and that will be there again the day after tomorrow, after peace has come, after all the toasts and embracing.

Where war is a serious thing, where it is a matter of life and death, there is no hatred. The more it becomes an irresponsible game, the more likely it is that hate will develop.

It is never there in the beginning.

What, within this structure, this setup, is the role of the press? Of public opinion? It is the intangible, that which is nowhere and everywhere, a mysterious mixture of honesty and lies, of the original and the artificially contrived, of the significant and the trivial. It is something on which the making of decisions sometimes must depend, and which at other times is overlooked and ridiculed—something dangerous and inconsequential at the same time.

Where, then is hatred—?

38

The full horror of certain eras can be recognized primarily by the fact that at such times that which otherwise appears to be the first precept of all morality can then come to be considered the greatest wrong—namely, to speak the truth.

Times in which truth can become dangerous not only for those who speak it but also for those who listen to it, are unwholesome at the core.

39

The state is a concern not of diplomacy but of the citizenry. In particular, it must not be the domain of a diplomacy that has for centuries been degenerating—by inbreeding, as it were. From this it follows that every state, a republic as well as a monarchy, is ruled in an absolutistic manner, in the sense that the fate of the countries is always determined by single individuals and that the voice of the people lacks any real importance—even though the people sometimes delude themselves, or are deceived into believing, that the opposite is true.

40

They say he died the glorious death of a hero. Why do they never say he suffered the magnificent mutilation of a hero? They say he has given his life for his country. Why do they never say he has had both legs amputated for his country?

(The semantics of those in power!)

The terminology of war has been coined by the diplomats, the military, and those in power. It should be revised by those who have come back from the war, by the widows, the orphans, the physicians, and the poets.

41

The most difficult thing in examining the question of war guilt is always this: to fit the world situation in the proper context, to know up to which link in the chain of causality one may go back without straying into infinity. Historically speaking, there is no state that is entirely without blame—that is as true for this war as it is for any other war.

Nevertheless, one would have to establish a

point in history from which to start in order to get a clear picture. In the coming peace negotiations it will be necessary to eliminate the question of guilt entirely. For once it has been broached, one would have inevitably to go back further and further, not only to mistakes in Austrian and German policy during the recent decades, but even to strained relations between countries (as for instance that between Austria and Russia during the Crimean War), to the negotiations at the Congress of Vienna, and even to the partition of Poland for which Catherine, Frederick the Great, and Maria Theresa were equally to blame and in which, if one wishes, one can also find another reason for the rivalry between Austria and Russia.

If one goes back still further, one will find that the desire for revenge on the part of France cannot be justified since, after all, Alsace and Lorraine were not taken away from the German empire before the time of Louis XIV. Going back further and still further, one comes to a period when France and Germany were really one and when the nations that exist today were neither ideologically nor politically adumbrated.

One could say that whatever has occurred between countries is stained by guilt, for, in the nature of things, all that happens in the realm of politics is, quite naturally, based on the right of the stronger. The so-called international law is nothing but an attempt to set against this law —the law that might makes right, a law that has been exercised for thousands of years—a law based on ethics; it is then only natural that it fails to work. International law—if it is to serve its purpose at all—can never become a reality until the rights of individual people are firmly secured. International law can never become a reality until the rights of the individual nations are fully safeguarded. Yet never before has it been so obvious as it is now that there cannot yet be any such rights, because, if for no other reason, the people themselves, in critical moments of their history, immediately divest themselves of their documented rights, partly from conviction, partly from suggestibility, partly from cowardice.

42

On the matter of this so-called "fated necessity":

Again and again we forget that that specific event which, post factum, appears to us as having been absolutely inevitable, inherent in the spirit of history or the will of God (depending on one's philosophy), was, before it occurred, no more than one of a thousand possibilities. Naturally, it had to happen in accordance with the law of causality, but often enough the final causal factor lay not on the main road of causality but rather emerged from a side path, and can therefore just as well be termed an accident, even though an accident is of course nothing but a necessity located off the main road that we are usually watching. One may state, therefore, that everything that has occurred happened metaphysically, i.e., inescapably, with the participation of all causalities operating from the very beginning, therefore by the will of God or by acts of fate—but that, logically, any event represents only that one possibility among a thousand that chance has selected.

That is the way we must think if we do not want to accept fatalistically everything that happens and is still to happen as the inescapable, the fated, the destined—and if we wish at all to reserve the right to rebel against that which seems to us unjust, senseless, and not a definitive solution. Otherwise we would have to be just as grateful for an unfavorable outcome as for a favorable one and could no more rejoice over a victory than be ashamed of a defeat.

43
※

Just as the continued existence of religious dogmas of all denominations and the continuing official domination of the churches do not prevent the scientist from continuing his investigations, even though time and again he arrives at results that contradict those dogmas; just as he certainly must not waste his time by engaging in a special fight against all those dogmas that will disappear from the world when their time comes as all preceding dogmas disappeared from the world and were replaced by new ones—thus the men who are working toward world peace, even toward eternal peace, or, rather, toward making war impossible, must not be thwarted in their work by the domination of the dogma of war: War is inevitable, decreed by fate; it is rooted in the organization of human nature. This dogma is false. War is inherent not in human nature, but in the way nations are formed and in the way in which individual nations relate to each other. The individual as such never wants war—at least not in the sense that through it he intends to bring about a new order of the political organization of the world. The exceptions are those for whom war is an opportunity to satisfy their personal thirst for adventure, their ambition, their greed, and those in whose interest it is—whether they be aware of it or not, whether it be in agreement with, or contrary to, their personal convictions—to keep up the dogma of the fated necessity of war. The total effort of the friends of peace must be directed at putting an end to the influence of these people, a task that, considering the fact that these people are in the minority, does not seem hopeless at all. War, even if it ends in victory, is always in the interest of only an infinitesimal minority. All problems that allegedly can only be resolved by war—i.e., disputes over borders (mostly only questions of dynastic power politics), problems of trade and national honor (prestige)—can always be settled also by different means. Thus the work for peace, viewed historically, will signify nothing else but another milestone on the road that democracy has to travel to its final victory over absolutism in its broadest sense. To me this seems to be the whole meaning of history. We stand only at the beginning.

44

So long as even one person exists to whom war can bring an advantage, and this one person has sufficient power and influence to unleash this war, any fight against war is in vain.

45

Unless the idea of peace wins out in all European states, simultaneously and completely, it merely constitutes a danger. If, for instance, nine out of ten states accept the idea of peace and reach the agreement not to wage war under any conditions, then the one state that is willing to wage war (or, more accurately, the government that has the power to incite its people to a war of aggression, for the people never want war) has won its game—just as one armed man is at an advantage against nine unarmed men and will, of course, force them likewise to take up arms.

Therefore, agreement among all nations is indispensable.

It is self-evident that this cannot be attained through peace conferences, especially if monarchs participate in them. One might think, rather, of a peace parliament, which, of course, would have to be continuously in session. But immediately questions such as these arise: Where to convene? In which language to negotiate? How can a subject of a given country, elected to such a parliament, relinquish permanently his national citizenship, as it were? No more should these parliamentarians be permitted to think of war as a solution than should in a national parliament a duel between party leaders be considered as a solution in cases of contention. Just as in the parliaments of the individual countries, everything would have to be decided by vote, and the outvoted party would have to acquiesce.

The questions that may come up fall into three groups: questions of borders, of trade, and of national honor. In other words, matters of dynastic ambition, of competition, and of prestige.

The honor of a state, however, just as that of an individual, can be violated only by itself, never by others.

Disputes concerning trade could be arbitrated by letting the more industrious, the more active, the more gifted party have the advantage. Here, too, shoemakers enticing away each other's customers do not resort to duels. Why then when nations are concerned should it be decided by blood whether it be Jerry or John Bull who is to sell his products to his neighbors?

There are tremendous difficulties, but they are all cancelled out by the one incontestable fact that nowhere in the world does the overwhelming majority want war and that this majority must prevail in the end over the small minority that either wants war or needs it. Of that minority only a tiny fraction would have to suffer from the disadvantages, dangers, and atrocities of war, if it came to that.

46
✣

Somewhere in the world there is a corked bottle. Within, it whirls, quivers, and bubbles in constant motion. And everywhere there is great fear that the bottle might burst and that its red-hot liquid contents as well as the flying splinters might cause havoc. By a strange law, however, the right to uncork this bottle is given to only a certain group of people, and the danger of being injured and killed by the escaping contents of the bottle increases in proportion to the distance between oneself and the bottle. So that precisely those who pay the least attention to the bubbling and hissing, and who do not care whether or not the bottle is uncorked, are the most exposed to far greater suffering through the uncorking.

47
✣

"Great times" are those during which the discoveries and inventions made in "little times" are exploited for the killing and mutilation of people as well as for the destruction of the values and works that originated during the "little times."

48

Only when I meet someone blinded in combat who, even at the price of his sight, would not renounce having actively and passively participated in these great times, then and only then shall I believe that it really was a great epoch.

49

They speak of the purifying effect of war upon the individual, in the sense that war is supposed to bring out qualities in man that would otherwise have remained hidden.

Such qualities are of no consequence in the soul's economy. It is quite immaterial whether bookbinder X, shoemaker Y, or bank clerk Z courageously exposes his chest to enemy bullets. When he returns home he will be precisely the same person that he was before, and he will again exercise all those qualities that have no connection with the experiences of war, the good qualities as well as the bad.

The real hero finds in his everyday life a hundred opportunities to prove himself.

One must not overestimate the significance of courage shown in the performance of one's occupation or of virtues that materialize as a consequence of special circumstances. Every physician, for example, imperils his life a thousand times in the course of his life. Nevertheless, the percentage of noble and brave men is no greater among physicians than, for instance, among lawyers. Occupational virtues have no significance—or almost as little significance as occupational vices—for the development of mankind. There is the occupational piety of the clergy, the occupational courage of the soldier, and by the same token there is the occupational lack of shame of the prostitute. The fact that opportunity can bring out all these virtues or at least help to develop them—just as it can all vices—indicates that the seeds of such virtues or vices either were first borne by the storm of events into the souls of people, or that the seeds of all virtues and vices exist already at the time of birth.

50

So long as war is considered a possibility at all—i.e., so long as there are professions based on the possibility of war, and even so long as there is just one person who can acquire wealth or increase it by means of war, and that person be one who has the power or the influence to bring about war—just so long there will be wars. Here and nowhere else must one come to grips with the problem of world peace—not in the realm of religious or philosophical or ethical motives. These are totally irrelevant. Neither to reason nor to compassion nor to honor can we appeal with the slightest hope for success. It is exclusively a question of so reconstructing the world that no person, not even a single one, be it in the country of friend or foe, has the slightest chance to improve his personal affairs through war. Impossible? So long as that is impossible the peace movement has not the faintest chance of success. Neither with profundities nor with sentimentalities will you touch either the hearts of the diplomats or those of the generals or those of the defense contractors.

51

It is crucial that out of the millions now risking their lives for the sake of ideals—for the sake of nationalist and capitalist ideals, or at best for the defense of their country—there later emerge some few people who will be willing to risk their lives for something that is even greater than the defense of their country, namely, for the liberation of mankind.

52

The motivation for all events is rooted deeply in human nature. What we usually believe to be causes are almost always pretexts that are being exploited. No Frenchman who believes that Alsace by rights belongs to France, no Russian who thinks that Russia must have free passage through the Dardanelles, no Englishman who considers Germany a dangerous rival for markets—none of them would, as a direct result of such reflections and convictions, be willing to have his little finger cut off, much less to sacrifice his sight, his life, his possessions, the lives of his children. War, as it were, is waged as an abstraction. The individual always exposes himself to personal danger only from individual motives—from the spirit of adventure or from ambition, but most frequently under a certain compulsion and a drive to follow the herd instinct.

53

There would be no objection, from any point of view, to piety, or to surrender to the will of God, or to faith (or to whatever else we wish to call this spiritual condition) if the persons afflicted with this condition did not so facilely raise or lower the level of their piety according to their whims or needs. One can observe this phenomenon in every discussion. Here is an example: Someone says to me: "The speech of Bethmann-Hollweg[18] was nonsense. Had he not made it, or had he delivered a different one, we could have peace soon." I: "Maybe so, but the entire war is also senseless." Replies the other fellow: "We cannot know that. That is hidden from us—we are not on the inside."

Then I answer: "Either we have the right to criticize and therefore to call a stupidity anything that according to our lights seems stupid to us—be it some detail or some complex issue —or we do not have this right. At any rate, it is completely impermissible to specify a line of demarcation and then to declare that we have the right to criticize in one case but do not have the right to do so in another. We are not on the inside—admittedly. But if the deeper significance of the war is concealed from us, then the deeper significance of any detail occurring in the course of the war also remains concealed from us, as for instance the significance of that Bethmann speech—and we cannot know what purposes, opaque to our human eyes, God or fate or providence pursued with this apparently stupid speech (which, conversely, may seem quite sensible to others). Or we credit ourselves with the ability to see beneath the surface. Then I would not know at which point this right to criticize, and therefore also the right to opposition, should be limited."

A discussion must at all times be subject to the same logical, one could say logical-religious, principles. But even the most pious occasionally take the liberty, where some detail is concerned, of differing with God, as it were. They at least hint that something could have happened differently, and that this different course would have been better. (It matters little that, to be on the safe side, they may add "unfathomable divine decision," or something like that). The nonpious, on the other hand, the rebellious, the revolutionaries, sometimes catch themselves assuming (especially when the outcome confirms their personal opinions) or suspecting that the course of the world is not absolutely senseless, that, rather, somewhere there seem to be operating justice, reason, and therefore a God. How is one to assume, however, that God, before whom everything is equally large or equally small, takes an interest in the whole, yet is not interested in the details, or that he tolerates the nonsense of the detail but is nevertheless concerned with the meaning of the whole? That is all the more inconceivable because, according to the law of causality, everything functions at the same time as cause and effect and because even a seemingly most unimportant detail can be of tremendous importance for the whole, just as a grain of dust can slow down, indeed can bring to a complete stop, the working of a gigantic machine.

54

The individual as such never wants war. He wants action (in a good or in a bad sense), danger, adventure, fame, glory; and he uses war as a means—as the most irresponsibly used means—for his purpose. For all of these, action and adventure, danger and glory, can also be attained in different ways, but discovering those different ways requires a greater mental effort and, primarily, a certain independence of thought. And one of decision.

Sometimes the individual as a citizen of his country does desire war, but if so, he wants it only as a defensive measure. And since the citizen of every country is indoctrinated with the belief that his country's war is a war of defense, he generally wants the war for as long as it happens to last.

The individual as a soldier subject to compulsory military service never wants war, for if he wanted it, there would be no need for compulsory military service.

55

The solidarity of those in power is much stronger than that of the peoples. It persists through the centuries. There exists (in a certain sense) a stronger affinity among the Roman caesars, the kings of France, and the czars than among proletarians of two neighboring nations living at the same time. The solidarity of those in power is a solidarity of an idea; that of the peoples, the solidarity of distress.

56

The era of Charles V.

He cannot wage war because he has no money.

The only solid and permitted basis of militarism.[19]

Stroke of genius of kings: Money is not always at our disposal, but we do have the power. Therefore, let us invent something new—compulsory military service. That comes cheaper for us. Let us make the citizens finance our soldiers, the fathers pay wages to their sons whom we send to their death.

We have no right to do that? Then let us invent the theory of the divine rights of monarchs.

Our soldiers do not know for what purpose they are going to their death? Then let us invent dynastic feeling.[20]

57

What wretches are those to whom this war has actually taught something new. They know as little of human beings as they ever really understood history. And technical progress as well as the necessity to figure with higher numbers so confuses their reason that they do not recognize that which has occurred time and again since the emergence of the human species and has yet always remained the same.

58

The individual has never wanted war. Perhaps he wants combat, adventure, entertainment, also profit, glory, danger. Sometimes he even wants someone else's death, someone else's misery. He may want murder, plunder, pillage (which may be committed with relatively the least personal risk precisely during a war). At best he wants victory, triumph, exaltation of his country at the cost of other people who live in a different country. No one would claim that an individual ever wants for himself injury, torment, hunger, disease, misery, destruction. Therefore he would not want war either if he were able to visualize how all these things—injury, etc.—would affect him as an individual.

It is precisely this lack of imagination that is exploited by those people who desire only profit or glory or thrills (not just adventure, let alone danger) for the purpose of getting the masses to believe that they desire war as such, as a struggle of army against army and of nation against nation. And as motives for this alleged desire of the masses, so-called violated national interests are conjured up for them, or some danger to their country and thus to themselves and their families—and finally the advantages of an expansion of their own country for reasons of prestige and business.

And if all these reasons are still insufficient for the fairly sensible, then the ideologists bring forth their so-called historical necessity. The latter, however, is the most ridiculous and sometimes the most infamous of all fabrications. History in any case, takes its course, and whatever happens will afterward be proclaimed a historical necessity. At least, no one has ever heard of historical superfluities. And why, then, do they pray to God? If there were a historical necessity —and this concept does actually fit into religious ideology—then it would necessarily be a firmly established fact since the very beginning of time. For the hypothesis that such historical necessities alternate with historical non-necessities cannot be reconciled in any way at all with a historical, a religious, or even just a logical view. Historical necessity—that is nothing but empirical causality. And no event can be predicted with mathematical certainty *before* it has actually occurred. God himself would not be able to foresee it—and, to be sure, the more he were God, the less he could do so.[21]

59

The military can easily exist without war. They would get along quite well with maneuvers. Only the diplomats are in urgent need of it.

60

Let the soldiers govern; then perhaps there will soon be an end to wars—at least for so long as the diplomats have not returned to power.

Editor's Notes

[1] The date 1904 was added in pencil to the original typewritten text and is not quite legible. While it is conceivable that the text originated after 1904, it is certain that this passage was written prior to the outbreak of World War I.

[2] This essay comprises eleven typewritten pages and constitutes Schnitzler's attempt to express, and thus clarify, his attitude toward the war that had just begun. The writing of this essay serves a combination of interrelated purposes: first, to reassert firmly those fundamental ethical convictions that related to the war; secondly, to bring clarity and order into the multitude of intellectual and emotional responses to the advent of the war, and, finally, to effect for himself a process akin to catharsis. Therefore, those passages that contain Schnitzler's private, transient, emotional thoughts—applicable, as it were, only to his personal state of mind in October 1914—are omitted here. Those passages, on the other hand, that reflect generally appli-

cable, permanent philosophical attitudes and thoughts are retained.

³ Dr. Josef Redlich, a university professor and member of the Austrian parliament, was a friend of Schnitzler's. This aphorism and the following (No. 8) are the only ones found that Schnitzler attributed to someone else.

⁴ The latter part of the last sentence has been reconstructed from a garbled version in the original transcript.

⁵ In line with the German *Dichter* the expression does not mean here lyrical poet but applies also to great prose writers.

⁶ Richard Dehmel (1863–1920), an important lyric poet.

⁷ Schmock was the name of a minor character in Gustav Freytag's comedy *Die Journalisten,* 1852. It is used here to designate an unprincipled journalist.

⁸ Karl von Clausewitz (1780–1831), a Prussian general and outstanding strategic theorist. A more complete version of his much-quoted statement to which Schnitzler refers reads as follows: "War is not merely a political act, but also a political instrument, a continuation of politics, a carrying out of the same by other means."

⁹ Several interpretations of the last statement are possible. Thus it may be that Schnitzler is thinking here of free will as an integral part of the dynamic principle immanent in Spinoza's *natura naturans*. He might also have thought that free will, being the activating force behind the creative ingenuity of man, has been the determining factor in the shaping of our present

world (not of the universe), that it is therefore an essential, innate property of man and cannot disappear without a fundamental alteration of man's psychical structure, resulting in a total paralysis of all selective activity. There are other possible interpretations. The important point here is the fact that Schnitzler employs the factor of free will to refute the theory of the necessity of war.

[10] By "compulsory military service" Schnitzler is probably referring not to mandatory peacetime training of citizen-soldiers for defense —which rarely constitutes a threat to the lives of the trainees—but to using them as involuntary cannon fodder in war, particularly in a war of aggression.

[11] The correct date of this passage may be 1919 rather than 1915. In the original transcript it appears on the same page with, and below, an item dated 1919.

[12] Small town on Austro-German border, which is used here as the equivalent of "Podunk."

[13] Romain Rolland (1866–1944), French novelist and dramatist, professor of the history of music (Sorbonne), winner of the Nobel Prize for literature (1915). At the beginning of World War I he decided to remain in Switzerland to facilitate his self-imposed task of integrating the pacifist work of the leading intellectuals of France, Belgium, and Germany. The arguments used in his unsuccessful attempts toward this end were collected and published under the title *Au-dessus de la mêlée*.

[14] In this essay of more than four single-

spaced typewritten pages Schnitzler analyzes Rolland's articles and concludes that even this man, from whom Schnitzler expected "justice and objectivity," hardly shows a trace of these attributes any longer. The details of Schnitzler's arguments are omitted here because they lead too far afield. His subsequent discussion is proof of the validity of his initial assertion that the question of war guilt must not be discussed during the peace negotiations. For if two such peace-loving, highly intelligent men of good will as Schnitzler and Rolland were unable to reconcile their views as to who or what was responsible for the war and its conduct, it would seem to follow that a group of diplomats and politicians—many of them undoubtedly less sincere and less dedicated to world peace—could never arrive at a satisfactory, let alone a just solution.

[15] See Nos. 6 and 49.

[16] The German original of this passage is in rhymed verse.

[17] In the remainder of this article Schnitzler examines the question of whether Germany had actually started the war. He expresses his conviction that, though Germany was responsible for the declaration of war and for the timing of its outbreak as well as guilty of a number of major political blunders prior to that time, her enemies were far from innocent and rightfully should share the blame. Note the accurate prediction (in the last paragraph) that the perception of the true nature of war as recognized in 1919 would not endure for very long.

[18] Theobald von Bethmann-Hollweg was Ger-

man Chancellor during World War I until 1917.

[19] A number of Schnitzler's notes were written in telegraphic style. This cryptic remark apparently refers to his conviction that only paid volunteers, i.e., career soldiers, should make up the armed forces of any country.

[20] The "dynastic feeling" is the loyalty of the subjects and their sense of obligation toward the ruling house of their monarchs. Thus, before the end of World War I, the Germans were supposed to have dynastic feeling for the House of Hohenzollern; the Austrians, for the House of Hapsburg; etc.

[21] Original: *und umso weniger, je mehr er eben Gott wäre* (and so much less, the more he *were* God). This is not to be construed as a denial of an all-knowing and all-powerful God. It indicates, rather, that Schnitzler's God concept was largely identical with Spinoza's. Not God's *existence* is denied. What is denied is the assumption that he would intervene in any manner in the course of a universe created to continue without further guidance and endowed, for that purpose, with all the necessary potentials. Schnitzler also denies that God would, in an analogous way, concern himself with the fate of mankind, let alone with that of individuals.

Like Spinoza, Goethe, and Einstein, Schnitzler saw man as a part of nature—not as something created outside of it—and God as the immanent *dynamic* principle of nature as a whole (*natura naturans*). Thus He was the object of reverence or "intellectual love" (*amor intellectualis Dei*), not a transcendent being who would interfere with His own natural laws. Hence Schnitzler's statement that God, if he really were God, could not foretell future historical events: doing so would necessarily constitute a violation of his own essence as the immanent principle of *na-tural* order in the universe, an absurdity. The assumption that such could occur would have been synonymous with the rejection of the entire God-idea in the pantheistic sense.